" We tend to look through language and not realize how much power language has.

- Deborah Tannen

Copyright © 2022 by Anne Mitchell.
All rights reserved. No portion of this book, except for brief review, may be reproduced, stored in a retrieval system, or transmitted in any form or by any means — electronic, mechanical, photocopying, recording, or otherwise — without the written permission of the author.

Author: Anne Mitchell
Illustrator: Suzanne King

ISBN: 978-1-7374438-4-1

Library of Congress Control Number: 2022908011

Published by:
Game B Press
Speedway, Indiana, USA
gamebpress.com

WE CAN SAY...

---

illustrated suggestions for inclusive, peaceful idioms

by Anne Mitchell
with illustrations by Suzanne King

introduction:
WHY PEACEFUL IDIOMS?

Idioms—short little phrases that we use day in and day out—have meanings that are not consistent with the actual words used. And we use idioms all the time. Most of us have no idea how often we use idioms. But start thinking about idioms and you'll notice them in your own and others' speech, so often it may shock you.

When Suzanne and I started talking about putting this book together, my husband and I started noticing how often we use and hear idioms. And how we normalize violence through the idioms we use. We are not even aware of how violent many of the idioms are.

Here is a very short list of some common idioms:

take a shot…	adding insult to injury…	right on target…
take a stab…	that really bombed…	bullet points…
a shot in the dark…	roll with the punches…	beats me…

All of these idioms mean something other than the words they use. Many of them mean to try something; to not know; to have something fail; to have something succeed. None of these idioms refer to *actual* physical or emotional violence. They speak to events in our daily lives that we equate to difficult, violent events and we use these idioms to get a point across quickly and succinctly. But at what cost?

What impact does using violent language have on us?
What impact does it have on our relationships, on our communities?
Why do we keep using battle and wartime analogies for every part of our lives? How does this keep us from attaining the peace and harmony we say we are looking for?

Suzanne and I are not research psychologists and we're not going to "prove" that the use of these idioms causes more violence in our lives. But we *are* going to use common sense to point out that the words we use matter. We know this when we think about any of the -isms: racism, sexism, speciesism. We have invented or used specific words to keep us separate from—superior to—whomever we are trying to oppress, consciously or not. So we *do* know that language matters.

And we also know that we have a choice. We can continue using violent language to express ourselves about nonviolent events. Or we can change our language to better reflect the world we want to inhabit. What might happen if we change violent idioms to more peaceful, loving ones? Might we bring more love, compassion and empathy into our world? We think so. We want to try. We think every little change moves us in the right direction.

In Cloud Atlas, David Mitchell said: "My life amounts to no more than one drop in a limitless ocean. Yet what is the ocean, but a multitude of drops?" And Rumi said: "You are not a drop in the ocean. You are the entire ocean in a drop." So perhaps using language that is full of love and compassion and empathy will move us to live in more love, compassion and empathy—for all life on this earth. Come join us!

instead of
"bigger fish to fry"

we can say...

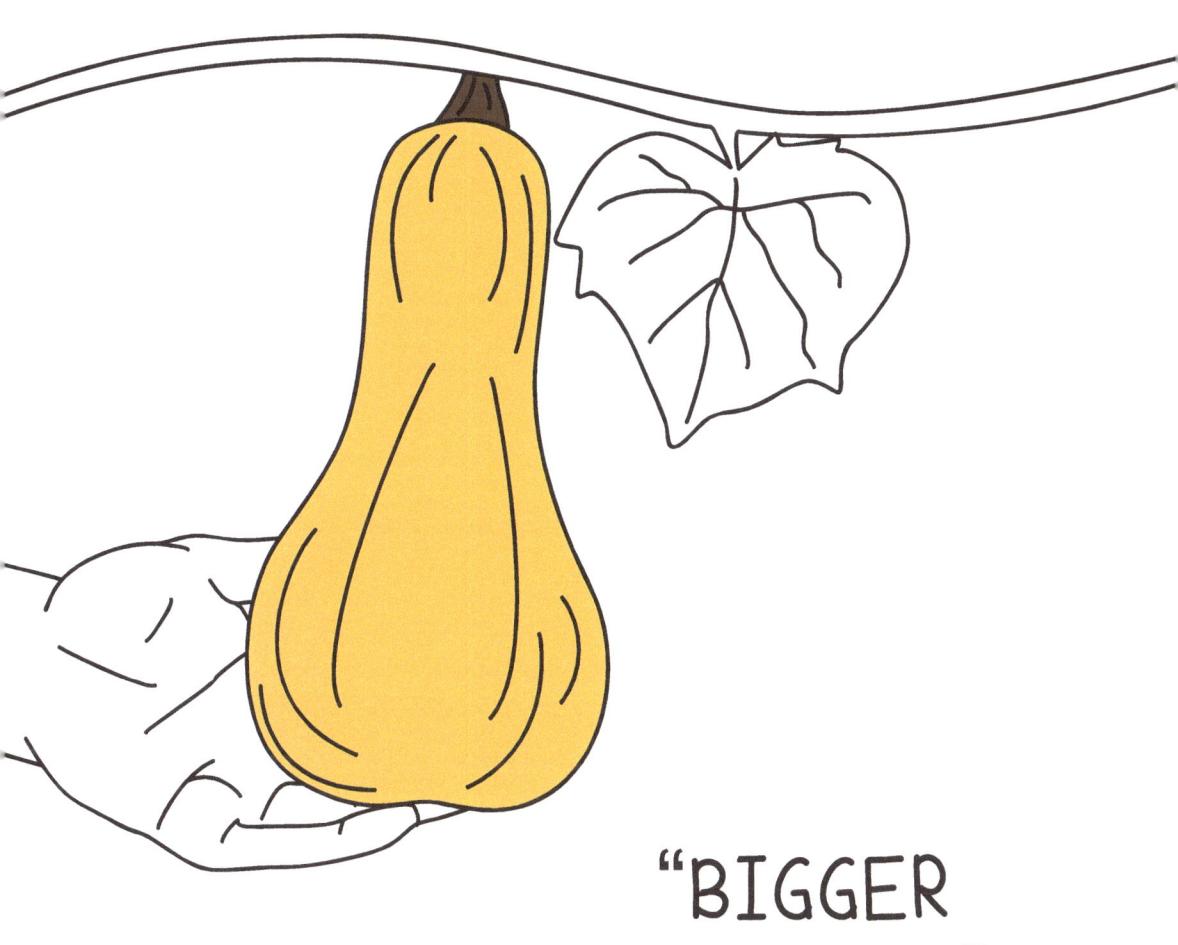

instead of
"kill two birds with one stone"

we can say...

instead of
"beat a dead horse"

we can say...

instead of
"don't count your chickens before
they hatch"

we can say...

 AMARANTH

 BUCKWHEAT

 CHICKPEAS

"DON'T COUNT YOUR SEEDLINGS BEFORE THEY SPROUT"

instead of
"bite the bullet"

we can say...

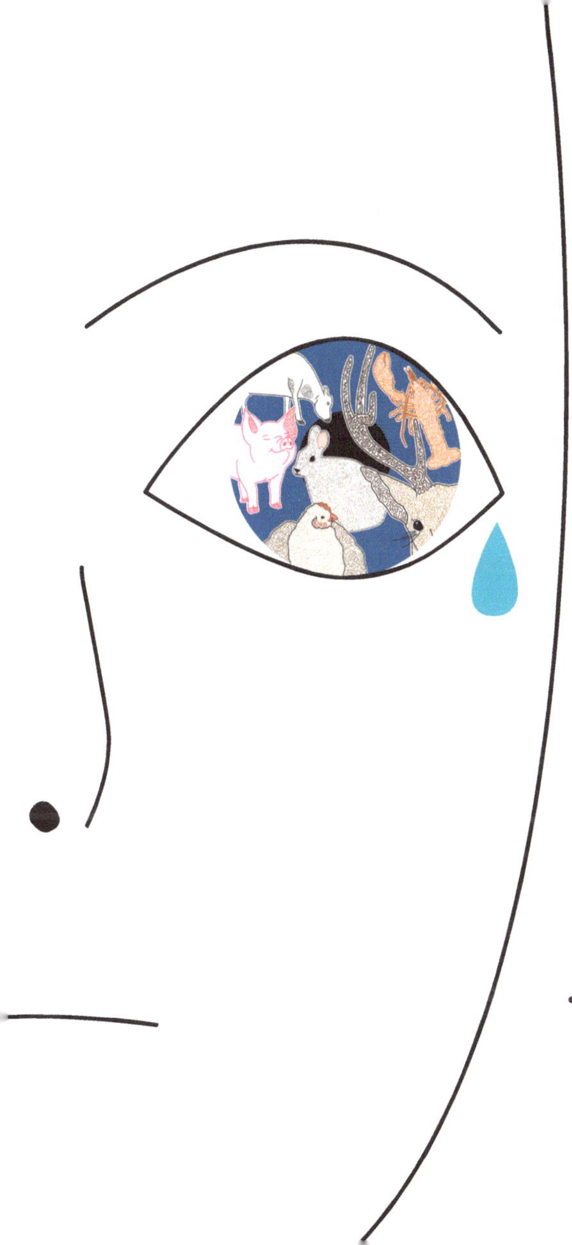

DUN
DUN
DUNNN

"FACE
THE MUSIC"

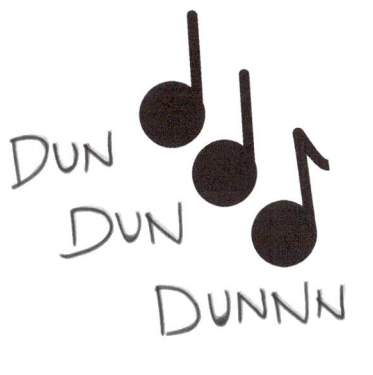

instead of
"you can't make an omelet without
breaking a lot of eggs"

WE CaN say...

instead of
"a deafening silence"

we can say...

"A GLARING SILENCE"

instead of
"take a stab at it"

WE CaN Say...

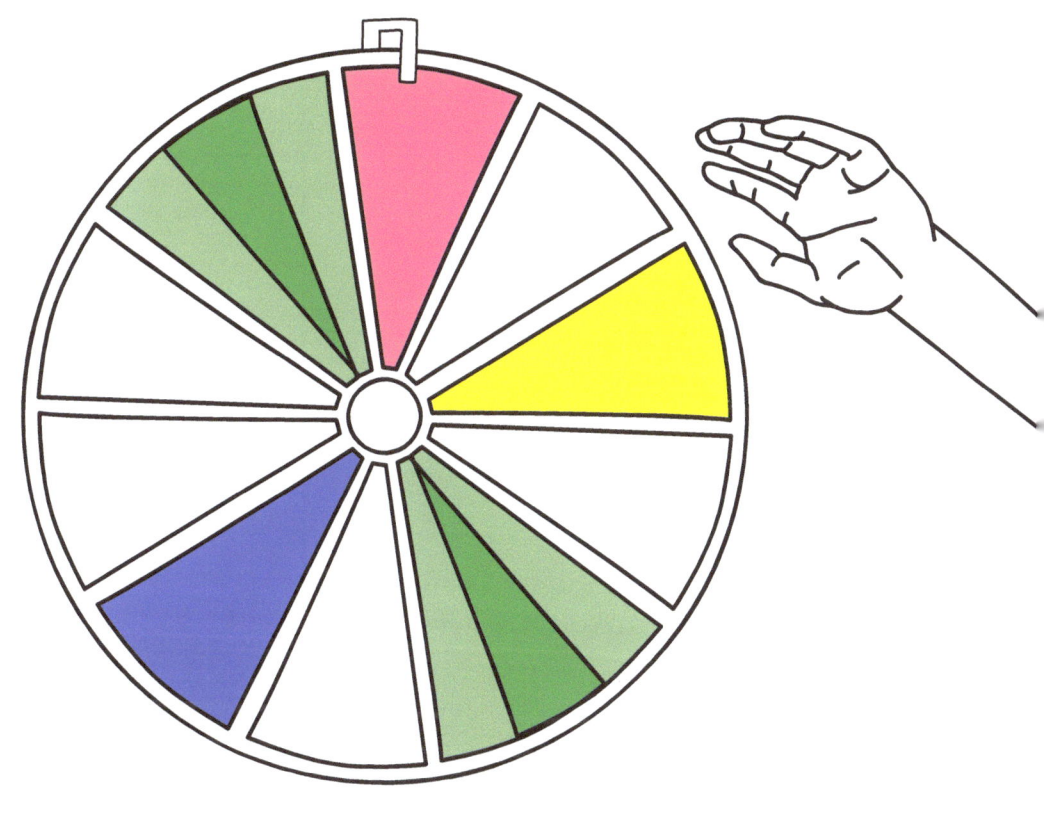

instead of
"more than one way to skin a cat"

we can say...

instead of
"packed in like sardines"

we can say...

instead of
"don't put all your eggs
in one basket"

WE CaN Say...

instead of
"give a man a fish,
　　　feed him for a day;
　　　　teach a man to fish,
　　　　　feed him for a lifetime"

we can say...

"GIVE A PERSON A VEGETABLE, FRUIT, OR GRAIN, FEED THEM FOR A DAY; TEACH A PERSON TO GARDEN, FEED THEM AND THEIR COMMUNITY FOR A LIFETIME AND BEYOND"

in conclusion:
WORDS MATTER

Words matter. Words have power. We know this as we have all been moved to tears by words, in happiness and in sadness. We have all felt exquisite joy from words, and we have been deeply shamed by words. Words have inspired each of us to act. Words really are a big deal.

We'd like to act that way with all the words we use every day. Not in some way that is limiting but in a way that is expansive, that promotes joy and health and diversity and fun. And we each control the words we use. But we don't often think about the idioms that are such a part of our everyday language. So let's think about them.

Let's consider the idioms we use, and let's change those that are violent to ones that evoke peace and serenity—or even silliness. We don't think this will create a more peaceful world all by itself. But we do think it will help to tilt the scale, to add a little bit of weight to the peaceful, loving side of life we would like to see more often.

If it is true that "words create worlds" as Pierre du Plessis said, then let's make sure that our words are creating the world we want to live in.

want t♡ see m♡re ♡f ♡ur w♡rds?
visit us at gamebpress.c♡m

draw your own alternative idiom and submit it at **gamebpress.com**

name: _____ date: _____

www.ingramcontent.com/pod-product-compliance
Lightning Source LLC
Chambersburg PA
CBHW040021130526
44590CB00036B/54